1

Carnal Sobriety

KATANDRA SHANEL JACKSON

Printed in the United States of America

Cover design by Elaina Lee
Final Proofs & Edits by RuleBreaker Editing
& Katandra Jackson Nunnally

First Printing, 2014
ISBN 978-0-9896786-6-7

FreedomInk Publishing
P O Box 1093
Reidsville, Georgia 30453
www.freedomink365.com

1. Psychology : Human Sexuality
2. Biography & Autobiography : Personal Memoirs
3. SELF-HELP / Compulsive Behavior / Sex Addiction

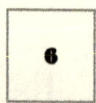

Acknowledgements

There was one that I sought refuge in as I embarked upon this mission. One that didn't think me crazy to swear off any cravings and indulging of the flesh. One that shall remain nameless. It was she that I confided in. Like some strange confessional. I gave her every update! "Hey guess what, I'm on day 3 of no sex!" "Hey guess what, I just could not resist!" "Hey guess what, I'm celebrating day 1 of no sex again for the umpteenth time!" It was she that celebrated with me and kept me strong just one more day and didn't chide me when I fell off the wagon and into the arms of that old addiction. Thanks CW, I owe you my sanity! I could not have made this journey without you.

Special Thanks

A special thanks to my husband who never shied away from the idea of this book. Who never once shunned me because of my past transgressions. Who loves me whole heartedly, unconditionally, without pause. Who accepts me and fulfills my every need. What addictions?

A very special thanks to Mr. Christopher John Farley and Dr. Helen Fisher for their personal permissions. I can honestly say that I can't imagine this book existing without the quotes you have both so brilliantly penned. Thank you.

Dedication

I dedicate this book to anyone that has or have ever had any type of addiction(s). You are not alone!

I also dedicate this book to the Non Fiction Authors of the World. Keep writing.

A Letter To the Reader

The idea of this book was born of all of those AA type books out there. Addicts work their way through the steps, the phases, the stages. It's a beautiful guideline. One that only an addict could truly appreciate. It helps to have the path marked before you. Makes it harder to deviate! So as I began composing Carnal Sobriety, I drew inspiration from this path! I allowed a once upon a time substance abuser to read what I'd written up to that point. He loved it, minus the 'religious' stuff. He remarked that addicts seeking to get clean get enough of that. What they need is real, raw honesty. He said my book would be so much better if I would just lose the heavy nod to the Bible. His suggestion has been taken into account and although while I will not dismiss The Most High completely, Carnal Sobriety will be gritty. Please take note that you've been warned.

Disclosure

I'm not the most religious person but I concede to a Higher Power. I do believe that One created us all. That this Higher Power has the last say in each of our individual fates. I also believe that every conscious being has inherited freewill. It's a most precious gift bestowed upon every man, woman and child.

Psalm 121 reads, "I will lift up mine eyes unto the hills from whence cometh my help. My help cometh from the Lord, which made Heaven and Earth."

Don't let the word 'help' fool you. Yes, we have freewill but God is the Captain of the vessel which is your life. He is in complete control once you relinquish the death grip you have over the helm!

Now I must warn you beyond my lack of religious scholarliness, most of the books I have researched on addiction refer to some type of drug codependency and the brunt of most of these books is comprised of passages and scriptures. I did utilize these books, the internet, personal acquaintances, the Bible, my own experience with addiction. But let it be said here before the book unfolds, that this is not another AA (Alcoholics Anonymous) book.

"I only know one way to write. The pen for me is a double edged sword. One side is brutally honest. The other side is beautifully marred with things that maim & murder! And I continue to chronicle my life in this series of ongoing, partial memoirs."

~Katandra Shanel Jackson

Carnal Sobriety

KATANDRA SHANEL JACKSON

WHERE TO BEGIN?

Webster's Dictionary defines addiction as a compulsive need for and use of a habit-forming substance such as heroin, nicotine, or alcohol, characterized by tolerance and by well-defined physiological symptoms upon withdrawal. A much broader definition paints addiction as the persistent compulsive use of a substance known by the user to be harmful.

Confession... I'm tired. Not physically tired. And despite all of the 'relationships' that I've been in and out of, I'm not emotionally tired. I'm spiritually tired! Tired of attempting to control a situation I clearly am not in control of. These addictions have overpowered me. They have become me. And I'm tired. I know it's time to ask A Higher Power to navigate these troubled waters from this point and forevermore. Something has to give. Either the way I'm living or life itself. I'm so very tired.

DEFEAT AIN'T EASY TO ADMIT

My name is Katandra Shanel Jackson and I don't need some professional shrink to tell me that I'm a sex addict!

From experience, I can honestly attest that it is the one with the problem who is usually the last to know. Those around you know something is amiss. Oh who am I kidding? We know! It's just not an easy thing to admit. It took me 10 years & 7 months to confess this truth to... Me!

Before setting off on this mission, I went into full research mode. Reading books, searching different websites, even conducting a very personal one on one interview with a recovering crack addict, who shamefully admits he's constantly in remission. The consensus [at least by published books on codependency] is that there are 12 steps to recovery. Recovery from being an alcoholic, a shopaholic, a chocoholic, a kleptomaniac, a meth, crack, cocaine fiend.

I don't wish to discuss in length what has been covered in those other books about addiction. This ain't another AA (Alcoholics Anonymous) book.

WHAT'S IN A NAME?

Nothing new under the sun. Everything has at least twice been done. Now doesn't that take some of the edge off of feeling all alone? Still when you are in the midst of that storm, every blow is the hardest.

I do not have a substance addiction. My addiction is behavioral. The latter I truly fear. I don't take lightly any addiction, but in my mind, if a person has a substance abuse addiction, they simply need to remove the substance and just like some magic wand being waved over the grim situation, everything is okay with the World once more. No more addiction! I know it's not that easy. I know someone that has or is currently battling a substance abuse addiction, must think I'm a stupid, dumb, naïve little girl. Living in a fairyland with unicorns and rainbows! I'd never make light of any addiction. To any substance abuse addicts out there that may have chanced upon this book, I do apologize. I repeat, this ain't another AA (Alcoholics Anonymous) book. However I do implore you to continue reading. It is my understanding that every addiction is born of some type of need.

A need to fill a void. A need to achieve that initial high. A need to feel accepted. A need that only another addict truly understands.

I read a quote once by Eckhart Tolle that states, "Every addiction arises from an unconscious refusal to face and move through your own pain. Every addiction starts with pain and ends with pain. Whatever the substance you are addicted to – alcohol, food, legal or illegal drugs, or a person – you are using something or somebody to cover up your pain."

Is that the ultimate need? To secure some agent to act as a salve, a bandage, a cover-up, concealer over the black eye, as opposed to facing the issue head on. Nobody wants to address the fist. We'd all much rather take something for the pain and make it all go away.

MY OWN PSYCHOSIS

Behavioral Addictions scare the hell outta me! I mean, I know it's not easy to break free of a substance addiction, but how am I supposed to rid myself of something so inherent, something so inbred as my own psychosis. Behavior... Isn't that like personality, characteristics? That stuff is embedded! It's in my DNA, deeply imprinted. Ouch!

The addictions that afflict me so endearingly complement one another. I believe without the onset of one, perhaps the other wouldn't even exist.

Every situation is unique. I'm almost opting to not date during this 'carnal sobriety'. But the approval dependent, absolute control freak, loser magnet, sex craving addict in me is telling my body that this is not a good idea.

APPROVAL DEPENDENCY

When we seek to be approved, not only are we seeking to please another, but we derive pleasure in doing so. No matter how brief or how fleeting the moment.

Chemistry, Biology, Physical science teaches us that the first high is the best high. That no matter how often you take a drug, you'll never again reach that initial euphoria. This could be the reason that marijuana is considered a 'gateway' drug. Because once those floodgates have been opened, you'll do almost anything in pursuit of that very first high.

It is the same with Approval Dependency. I feel the need to please people is embedded not just in our individual psyche's, but our collective genetic makeup as well. For me, this one addictive agent has bled into another. It's not uncommon for one addiction to lead to another or for two or more addictions to coexist and overlap. It's kind of hard to say which came first. The chicken or the egg. So is the case with my addictions! Approval dependency. Sexual addiction. Control addiction. Dependency on toxic relationships. Are you seeing how one can bleed into and become and encourage another?

On the outside looking in, I'm the one calling the shots. But the truth is, my spirit is in a constant state of turmoil. I'm an emotional wreck to say the very least. Life is a delicate dance. We live in a society that governs we all get along. The invisible fine print, the unwritten rules and regulations state that we appease to each other's nature and in doing so, we by nature, seek to please. This thought alone leaves me to ponder a very important question... Are we all born approval dependent?

ONE HAS GIVEN BIRTH TO MANY...

Sexual Addiction.
Control Addiction.
Dependency on toxic relationships.

They may seem as if they have nothing in common with one another, let alone relate to Approval Dependency. Remove your attention from these pages and think about it. Place yourself in the shoes of the one who seeks to please. With that first high of pleasing another, the grounds for Approval Dependency is set. A Sexual Addiction has been birthed before you realize that it was even conceived. You seek to please sexual partners because you think this is the way to be approved. Actively seeking for these sexual partners places you in a mindset of being in control. The Control Addiction sets in but sadly because the state of being in control is purely a mirage, you remain in a forever state of actively seeking for sexual partners, the need to be approved in this manner becomes a serious thing. Along with the Sexual Addiction & the Control Addiction, you've created in your mind's eye, an image of the perfect mate. But no matter how often you submit yourself into relationship after relationship [And I do use the word 'relationship' loosely only because sex is always involved and usually comes into play way before a true 'relationship' has been established. Sometimes a solid friendship hasn't even been forged] lovers, they come and go.

A plethora of sexual partners that 'love' you and leave you, are the side effect, an indirect result of the initial addiction; Approval Dependency. Now everything about your aura begins to attract those truly unworthy of your time; Dependency on toxic relationships. But you insist that it is truly you that is in control; Control Addiction. The Sexual Addiction becomes even more surreal as sex becomes the precursor to love, not the other way around and every toxic relationship leaves its mark on the timeline of your life & ultimately your heart...

HE LOVES ME. HE LOVES ME NOT…

Every guy has his thing. *Tom liked loud music. *Dick liked fast cars. And *Harry had a thing for the finer things in life. He especially loved fine dining. And five star restaurants? Forget about it! He knew every Sous Chef by name! Video games. Comic books. Cinema connoisseurs. And they all had a passion for the same woman... Me. Woman, how loose can thy art be? With less than 2 weeks of physical contact, I had bedded each.

Some men prey on the feeble of mind. They can smell weakness like some kind of sick scent. It is the stench of broken things. It is the aura of that which needs repair. The smell is unmistakable. It screams, "Hey! Yes you. Insert yourself into my life riiiiiiight here!" as if I don't already have enough troubles.

BACKSTORY

This book was born of my own addiction, as you may have guessed by now. Those that know me best can bear witness that on occasion, I've been seen enjoying a glass or two of Port during festive times. I even partake in a drink or two at home. But I've never been one to overindulge in drink... And I've never done drugs. Except that one time I tried marijuana and hated the way it made me feel. And that one time I sniffed baby powder and hated the way that made me look. Dumb & stupid. These senseless things were done in the presence of a man, an ex, a not so distant but certainly a mere memory! The need to please [others & yourself] will make you do some crazy things.

I consider myself to be well versed in a plethora of topics and conversations, but a knowledgeable authority of narcotics I am not! So it is established. I do not have a substance abuse addiction, although the premise is derived of a common platform.

Several years ago, a particular book came to be in my possession. 'Serenity: A Companion for Twelve Step Recovery'. It was rarely and oddly one of those books that I just wasn't interested in reading. I don't have an addiction so a desire to read the book just was not present. However, because I'm such a book lover, I just couldn't bring myself to get rid of the book. So the book came into my possession. Sat on the bookshelf. Packed & unpacked with several moves over the years. Unread until one day...

A recent relocation has me deciding once again, which books to display and which to leave in boxes. My hands found this book and everything around me ceased for the moment to exist and I instinctively began to read the book. What I discovered almost instantly is that I was being indeed naïve. Here I am thinking I'm semi perfect. No addiction wracking my body. Sadly, I've been misinformed. Although usually referring to drugs, the definition of addiction goes much deeper than that. An addiction is any compulsive dependency on a substance, thing and/or activity [alcohol, marijuana, cigarettes, cocaine, crystal meth, chocolate, gambling, shopping, toxic relationships... Sex].

My guess is, there are a lot of people unaware that they have been harboring some compulsive dependency. Popular consensus states that there are 12 steps to recovery. Step 1 is admitting defeat. Repeat after me...

I am powerless. I have lost control. This addiction has taken over. The Nile is a river. So is denial. It courses through the veins of the addict not yet willing to admit defeat.

BACKSTORY CONTINUED...

Raised by a single mother. Molested by an estranged father. Taught that sex was the equivalent of love. They are one in the same. To get the latter, you had to freely give the former. Manipulated by an older boyfriend. Mind games were introduced to prove my love. Sex was a sure way to gain that love. Sex was a sure way to control that love. I became a statistic. Teenage pregnancy and a High School dropout. Abandoned by my firstborn's father. I began looking for love in all the wrong places. I became impatient in my search. Bypassing being friends and dating. Sex was the only item on the menu. My body was the buffet...

"Romantic love is an addiction."
-Helen Fisher

If romantic love is an addiction, I wonder what detriment the illusion of love will do.

"Every form of addiction is bad, no matter whether the narcotic be alcohol or morphine or idealism." -Carl Jung

MISDIAGNOSED

Shame in the name. Too many are being misdiagnosed and untreated! Drug and alcohol addiction is serious business. So it is the same with every addiction. The road to recovery is a road that you'll travel for life. Addicts, no matter their choice of substance, be it drugs, alcohol, sex, shopping, pleasing others, addicts often seek refuge in the company of other addicts.

There is no shortcut to recovery and no two people, no matter how similar their situations, will recover via the exact same route. However, there is preset before us, a very special set of steps, 12 to be exact, that will point you in the right direction of sobriety.

ADDICTED TO S-E-X

Let's not sugar coat it or beat around the bush. The prognosis ain't pretty. What an embarrassing addiction. Addicted to flesh, climax, sex! Every addiction inadvertently takes on the role of parasite and the host becomes codependent to the point that the addictive agent is beyond a want. The brain is tricked into believing the thing is needed. A sort of symbiotic relationship is formed. You are no longer in control.

"Dependency is a disease and every addiction needs a host." -Katandra Shanel Jackson

According to most books on addiction and recovery programs, there are 12 steps to wade through before reclaiming your sobriety. First we must declare that we have been overcome! Ok, it's sink or swim time.

NO LONGER IN CONTROL

Step 1: Admit defeat! In order to do so, one must:

I. Dismiss fear. Do not be afraid to loosen the reigns of the thing that actually has YOU by the throat. Remember, you're not in control. Let that beast go!

II. Relinquish denial. The sooner you admit defeat and stop denying that there is indeed a problem at hand, the sooner a solution can be found.

III. Place distance between yourself and like company. There are some in life that you cannot avoid. But don't go out looking for the hand that feeds your addictive need. Steer clear. Just say no!

Every ex is like a dealer serving my favorite brand of drug. They know what I like & how I like it and each is all too willing to give me what I want! It may seem free, the parting of legs, but it comes with a heavy price to pay...

In your hands I'm a mess. My body screams for sex. And you are all too willing to oblige. My knees your body pry. As you thrust into that sacred part of me. This desire, this need, this addiction is obviously stronger than I'll ever be!

Father God I am powerless without you. I have lost control. This addiction has taken over. Please take up residency in my body, heart and mind. Fill the void the addiction used to. Course a new river through these veins. I will not be afraid. I will not deny this acknowledgment. I will not defy that you are God.

CONCEDE A HIGHER POWER

Freewill is ours. The choice, the decision, the desire to begin this journey to recover is yours. But this battle once faithfully waged is the Lord's!

Step 2: Acknowledge a Higher Power.

"I admire anyone that rids themselves of an addiction." -Gene Tierney

It is you that must admit defeat and begin this journey, but no man or woman is an island. A journey of this magnitude is going to take some navigating. These are choppy, unchartered waters. The Creator is the Captain.

WHAT A PRECARIOUS PREDICAMENT

I felt like I needed a man to validate my worth. Sex made me feel wanted, needed, desired, beautiful, powerful, loved. I was totally in control. Right?

The goal at the start of this mission was to steer clear of compromising situations. I can only imagine that an alcoholic serious about kicking the addiction would not without great pain and some bonafide willpower, walk nonchalantly into a bar. Why then place yourself in compromising situations when seeking recovery from any addiction? These situations vary greatly. How to determine if you've put yourself in that precarious predicament? That's much easier than it sounds. You'll know because you'll feel at war with yourself! Your higher conscious, your moral self and your 'carnal' being, a.k.a your flesh, will be in a state of unrest! What should be a simple decision making moment becomes monumental. What you choose could be pivotal in this journey. So I've come to decide that I can't do this alone...

Step 3: Appoint a Higher Power.

So this destination is not where I planned to be. Since I've gotten so far off track and it seems I'm no longer even driving on the right road, I'm relinquishing all control. I'm switching off the engine. Getting out from behind this broken steering wheel. I think I'll buckle up and ride on the passenger side for a while. At least until this wilderness becomes familiar scenery again. Okay God. Take the wheel!

WHO NEEDS 'EM?

I've discovered sex without the heartache. But before we go there. If I may paint the scene. You know the one in which that moody, yet awfully handsome guy, decides to quit drinking. So he goes through his house with a trash can disposing of every visible and well stashed bottle of booze not so much in plain sight. Think, Denzel Washington in 'Flight'.

I dated this guy once that said often, "There is no perfect person. Only perfect intentions." Some people believe in a gradual abstaining when dealing with addictions. I know without a doubt, that a slow weaning will not be my chosen route.

I'm ashamed to admit it, but I do confess, I'm a sex addict. Relationship after relationship, I used to claim this excuse as the mantra of my heart... "I fall fast. I fall hard." But the truth of the matter is this, there's always sex to be had when there was a new man on the scene. And if we had sex, and we always did, it meant he loved me. Oh, what a recipe for disaster. Back to back relationships. That's my thing. As long as there's a man around, I never have to fear any sexual withdrawals...

I've discovered sex without the heartache. Mind you, for a very long time I needed a man to provide those 'carnal' needs. Then the day came when I purchased it...

"She goes from one addiction to another. All are ways for her to not feel her feelings."
~Ellen Burstyn

How can my addiction be sated without a man? That's just it. It can't! Or can it?"

OKAY I CONFESS. I LOVE SEX

I've had sex every day for the past 10 years. Either with a boyfriend, fiancé, husband, some temporary lover or myself. The birth of my last child commenced a different level of sexual addiction.

To ensure that my last child was indeed my last child, I underwent a micro-surgical procedure called a tubal ligation. I got my tubes tied. No more Ms. Egg meet Mr. Sperm and the two make baby! Nope I was done! Finish. Out of the baby making business. The electricity was off. No more bun baking going on in my oven. Without the worry of pregnancy I was free to have all the sex I wanted. I was the proverbial kid in a candy store. But sooner or later you're bound to come across a bad piece. I feared much more than rotten teeth and tummy aches.

As it goes in small towns, I was running out of safe options and sexual partners were growing scarce. So I purchased a massager. It was by no means made to be a sex toy but the vibrating head meant for shoulders and other aching body parts was purchased for the sole purpose of dousing my sexual needs. It would suffice until the next man found himself in my bed and between my legs.

Monday through Friday. Weekends. Yes Saturdays and Sundays too. No day was holy. Sex became my religion. I sacrificed my soul for those Earth shattering minutes. Every day I locked myself away from the world. My goal? An orgasm at any cost. My vibrator was my best friend. It knew what I needed. It was what I needed. My dependency grew so strong that it became near impossible to reach climax with a temporary lover.

A QUADRUPLE THREAT

Headache.

Heartache.

Hell.

HIV.

I can only think of one fate worse than Hell. For me that would be living a life with HIV because I slept with the wrong guy, got caught up in the moment, was careless. The headaches and the heartaches although unwanted are at least bearable. But if I continue to allow this addiction to take control over me, I'm afraid I'll be unable to finish composing this book. Let alone make a genuine attempt at this journey. Something has to stop and I refuse for that thing to be my heart!

Step 4: Assess the situation. YOU are the situation. A thorough Self-Evaluation is in order and long overdue.

My eyes are wide open. I see. I am fully awake. Now that my erroneous ways have been uncovered within me, there is no excuse for this madness to continue!

MIRROR, MIRROR ON THE WALL

No matter how ashamed I am to admit that I'm some sick, sadistic, strange, sex craving addict, I must do just that!

Step 5: I must authenticate these truths by being honest with myself, A Higher Power and at least one other soul.

I have designated a Check In Buddy! A trusted confidant who knows my struggles as I have laid the truth, the whole truth and nothing but the truth in her hands! She has agreed to be on constant stand-by. I have promised to contact her daily with a 'carnal sobriety' update. If you're stepping out on faith and have boldly decided to walk these steps with me, please please please I admonish, if you don't do another thing on this purging of the body, mind and soul, I implore you to do this... Be honest! If not with yourself, at least be truthful with your Check In Buddy. Make certain that the individual you choose for this task is:

1) Up to the job of being somewhat your Keeper.

2) Someone you trust and have no qualms with confiding in.

3) Someone that loves you, has your best interest at heart, will never judge and is all for helping you kick this addiction!

SOMETHING'S WRONG WITH THIS PICTURE

There was a time when sex made me feel weak, dirty, and powerless. I had no control over what was taken. My abuser made me ashamed of the most precious part of me. That which makes me a woman. I was just a girl!

I connect sex with feelings and feelings with love. Even my abuser fell hypnotic to the trance he set. He intended to be in control, but in the throes of climax after climax after climax (he was always rewarded with an orgasm and I began to punish my body by blocking the very sensation) the dynamics of the trance began to change. The act of malice was being tempered by what he felt each time he touched me. He fell in love with me. Not as a father adores his newborn daughter the first time he sees her sweet angelic face. His eyes reflected the amour men have for their wives, their significant others, their girlfriends, their Lover.

Having him wrapped around my little finger was no longer a daughter's deepest desire. He was enraptured between the legs that wrapped themselves around the very seed which assisted in the creation of me. A monster of his own making. Each orgasm I felt him growing weaker and in a sense my birthright was restored. In the very least, it was I who was finally in control.

CAUSE & EFFECT/AFFECT

Some fathers instill in their daughters high self-esteem, family values & overall good morals. I inherited a desire to please through sex. I'll never understand the reason why those we love & have been given the rights and responsibilities to love & protect us, I'll never understand the reason they hurt us! Perhaps we are all terminally ill. This disease is the 'Human Condition'. Why should I be ashamed of that?

Since the age of sexual activity, I have not abstained from the act of, for any significant amount of time. Three weeks, a month, max! Even in the absence of a man, my vibrator saw plenty of action... Daily in fact! This task, this revealing of such hard and ugly truths, is not done without much effort. This journey is of the flesh and the spirit.

NO MORE SEX

Exactly 28 days later, 4 weeks to the date, and I'm in another's embrace. On a euphoric high, spiraling down, down, down the rabbit hole of like to love in the amount of time it takes two to get naked. I suppose I never got the memo. Sex does not have to be an immediate condition of a new relationship. My body doesn't agree with this. So I've decided that the only way to abstain from sex is to abstain from men altogether. This is day 1 of my Carnal Sobriety. Cold turkey. No more indulging the desires of the flesh. Absolutely no sex!

Father, I pray for the strength to see this day through. Please guide my walk as I embark upon Day 1 of no sex. No sex of any nature. Not with a momentary lover or even myself. Please give me the courage to dispose the vibrators. Help me to rid myself of these temptations and let man not lead me back into those dark and desolate places.

I'm certain that liquor is not the best diversion for this night. However, it's keeping me company. Day 1. Night 1.

Father I pray for the strength to see this day through. Please guide my walk as I embark upon ANOTHER day of... Yep you guessed it... Carnal sobriety. No sex! Of any nature. Not with myself or with a temporary lover. Thank you in advance for the courage to seek you. Let man lead me not into temptation. My sexual addiction is no longer in control. You are! I lay my sobriety and my life in your hands. Amen.

THAT... WAS INSIDE OF ME?

A lack of sex has unleashed a plethora of dirty poems. Like a dam spilling over with nowhere else to go. Each filthy piece of prose has found my mouth a most inviting place!

'I Like The Way It Tastes In My Mouth' The sensation against my lips. The way it grows when caressed by silken fingertips. The way it moves me to mountain peaks. Driving me beyond the brink of ecstasy when it's deep inside of me. Reverberating against the walls of my soul. Eyes closed. Mouth prepared to shout... Your name... When whispered or spoken aloud. I like the way it tastes in my mouth...

'First Encounter' Panties pulled to the side. Your face buried nose deep. Your lips and mine meet. You caress my pussy with your mouth. You whisper secrets to her as I clutch the sheet. Intensifying the moment. She talks back to you. The two converse as if they've met before this night. Perhaps you stole away to my bedchamber in another lifetime. And the conversation carries on in the present as if I could be anyplace else. You speak in tongues and what was barely audible becomes shouts. Verbal and mental. As my love pours out. On this bed. Remembering the first time we 'met'...

I've got a serious case of sex on the brain! I've been touching myself in my sleep. Even in my subconscious dwellings the beast controls me. We may need an Exorcist!

Why for the love of Mary, Joseph and Christ, am I so hard pressed to find love beneath the chiseled flesh of man? I'm praying for an intervening divinity. Learning to love myself first and foremost is imperative at this point! Lost in the wilderness. No cookie crumb trail leading back. The compass needle in my heart, severely damaged. A Psychologist would need a Psychiatrist to emerge unscathed from the emotional sea I'm clearly drowning in. I'm not so sure prayer is going to be enough... What in the hell is wrong with me? Three weeks no sexual activity. I feel broken, battered, bruised. Like some very important bits and pieces are missing.

Step 6: Acceptance is key. Now is the time! We've admitted defeat. Acknowledged a Higher Power. Appointed that Higher Power. We've assessed the situation from within. We've authenticated these truths. Now is the time to accept that Higher Power. New Management is underway! Prepare the temple. Ready the battleground. We must arrange our actions and thoughts so that we may accept whole heartedly without a trace of rejection. New management is underway! It's been dark for far too long. It's the dawn of a new day.

NULL & VOID THE PAIN

What happens when the abrupt absence of one addictive vice adopts another? Brandy on the rocks. Straight. No chaser. What a way to ebb away the ache. Make it all go away. Withdrawal is serious business. It helps to not think about sex. Read. Write. Spend time with the family. Occupy my mind with thoughts other than the sweet relief of orgasmic release. I pray I don't pick up the habit of smoking cigarettes to take my mind off of that which is missing... Maybe liquor will null & void the pain!

"... a good, strong bottle of rum, when the heart is shattered and lonely, is always ample substitute for a lover's touch."
-Kingston by Starlight
(Christopher John Farley)

RELAPSE

A month long rendezvous and a two night stand prompted a new perspective. It has been my experience in life thus far that men only come for one thing, and that thing has never been my heart. Why should they start seeking something different? Because I am the one who has been settling. It's time I want something different, more, better for Heaven's sake & my sanity!

To begin again is to admit further defeat. I'm sick of feeling like a failure. I'm determined to be victorious in this journey. This is the reclaiming of self and a brand new day...

A NEW DAY

Around about 2 a.m every morning, I'm reminded of how I've allowed the addiction to please my flesh, to enslave me in this sexual rapture. Day 1 turned into Day 1 AGAIN! Shaky hands mark off the days triumphantly. One by one. 7 days is equivalent to 1 weak. No typo nor pun intended.

I walked into this New Year with a clear head, a clean heart and a body unclaimed. I made it through two weeks. Kind of helps that I'm in between boyfriends. Then it happened. The resurface of an ex. I'll spare you the sordid details of the impromptu indiscretion. Let's just say that I've been sexually sated. Now to begin... Again. I'm not certain I have the will to endure a new day.

Step 7: Let go & Let A Higher Power Take Control. Two traveling in opposite directions cannot both be in charge. One is bound to wind up lost.

Father dwell in me and remove these desires of the flesh. I am more than my body. I am more than sex. I place my life in your hands. Fix the broken pieces. Make me whole again. Please remove ALL of my flaws. Psalm 139:14 I am fearfully & wonderfully made. Marvelous are thy works. Father I come before you, humbly asking that you make me over. Take control.

TOO MUCH SELF-LOVE

Self-love is important in this journey of the flesh. The Most High does want me to love myself, right? I wonder if those who have taken a solemn oath to abstain from sex, like Monks & Nuns, I wonder if they are allowed self release.

It's time I define what the word 'sex' means to me. Put rather bluntly, sex to me is penile penetration. For a man to enter my vagina or anus with his penis. The desired outcome is NOT an orgasm. At least for me it's not. Sex is my feel good drug. It makes me feel wanted, needed, desired, yearned for, accepted, loved! Also, sex for me is any act where pleasure aid manipulation comes into play. Vibrators, massagers, dildos, any instrument whose sole purpose is to deliver me into ecstasy. The desired outcome IS an orgasm, no matter how brief or fleeting the release! Just the thought of driving myself to that point with a vibrator, excites me. The Earth stands still and everything ceases to exist as I near that peak. The rush is intoxicating. I crave it. I yearn for it! Then I remember, I got rid of those old vices. Now what?

Midnight musings and shower delights. No man, no vibrator, I suppose I'll just have to sex myself. I have double digitally thrust myself into a full minute of abandoned bliss. My body is in awe. Is this what self-love feels like?

ALIVE

Just what is the addiction, really? Sex? Climax? Power? Total abandonment? Interlaced and comingling, these addictions have cultivated at the very core of me. This joining, this union, this marriage of pain is affecting a Nation. How many will suffer? I wonder if it's the pain we're all addicted to. To feel something is better than to feel absolutely nothing. In the very least, pain is a reminder that no matter how screwed up I may be on the inside... At least I'm alive.

Step 8: Make a list of those we need to apologize to and amend the hurts inflicted by yours truly. Rather as a direct or indirect result of my addictions.

On the surface, it would seem that the only one that I've hurt is myself. But when I look deeper, the rabbit hole seems to have no end. I've hurt my children by allowing a steady stream of unsteady men into our lives. I've hurt my mother by not living up to the wish to have a better life than she & the generations before her. I've hurt the men that I've accepted in and out of my life as simply lovers and nothing else when I deserve so much more, by allowing each to use and abuse me. In and out of me, literally. My temple totally defiled. I need to apologize and make amends to my own body.

FOLLOW-THROUGH

Don't just make the list. See to it that those apologies have been made. Say it and mean it. It is another step in the process of righting the wrong and releasing the shame that is so readily attached to any addiction.

Step 9: Apologize to those you've made a list to make amends to that were hurt while you were under the spell of addiction.

*Use your judgment and only make those personal amends when the situation is safe to do so. If you're a Sex Addict and you're out there doing some weird, strange, freaky stuff, you may not want to revisit those places or faces. Apology or not! In the very least, apologize to yourself!

THE BATTLE WAGES ON

Take a look. Look harder. Look longer. Don't stop looking? What do you see? A much stronger you. Now look beneath the war paint. The old you is buried inside of the new you. Your memories, experiences, the fiend whispering out to you for that old vice. A battle has been waged. If I don't understand another thing about this journey, I know this, once you're an Addict, you're always an Addict. With willpower at hand and faith intact, any of us flawed creatures can remain sober.

Step 10: Continue taking inventory. The self-evaluation needs to be approached as a reoccurring, ongoing thing. Don't stop!

THE PATH HAS BEEN REVEALED

Now that the brambles and briars have been cleared from the path, I will not deviate from it. Life may at times throw a curveball and force me to reroute. But my destination is the same.

Step 11: Seek the continuation of this right path through a Higher Power. Pray and meditate for the will to carry on.

WIDE AWAKE DOT COM

How are you going to help somebody if you don't tell somebody? I'd never wish for such an embarrassing, hurtful, power rendering thing to have been all in vain. This pain has not been for nothing. I'm going to tell the world that all sorts of addictions do exist and of them, sexual addiction ain't no walk in the park. A lay under the swings or a quick romp under that great big oak, maybe. But it's no walk!! This journey for me has been a slow crawl. One that truly began because I told somebody. That same somebody that didn't believe me. Denial and that river. I had to convince ME that something was terribly wrong.

Step 12: The last step is simple. Tell & Testify! Okay, actually, Step 12 is just as difficult as the first where we admitted defeat, loss of control and the fact that this addiction had taken over! It's not going to be easy telling people that you're not perfect. Actually, it's going to hurt like hell to reveal these bitter truths! But in order to keep the testimony of your sobriety, you've got to give it away!

AFTERMATH

After I began the composition of this book and before its release into the world, I met a guy. Not just any guy. I wasn't looking for him. I was too thrilled at the joy of having found myself during this journey. And rumor has it, he wasn't looking for me! We were just two people that had been hurt, mostly because of the situations we allowed ourselves to get caught up in. The last thing to cross our minds before that magical meeting, was love. But what fate has in store cannot be messed with. He and I met and despite having been hurt so badly in the past, we did fall in love. A few short months later he took on my demons and I took on his last name!

Am I still a Sex Addict? I'm not too ashamed to admit that I am. I have a beautiful, intelligent, caring, considerate, sexy piece of man slumbering beside me nightly. He is my favorite drug.

P.S. That old crutch has made its way back into my life. But this time those AAA batteries are stocked for fun. My husband is patient and oh so passionate. I've found my 'O'.

The End.

"*Those who love tragic nonfiction are like bystanders of a bloodbath! Life is full of malice. Scars remind those looking on, that we're all beautifully imperfect human beings. Marvelously flawed are we!*"

-Katandra Jackson Nunnally

ABOUT THE AUTHOR

Katandra Jackson Nunnally is the CEO of FreedomInk Publishing. She spends her time delicately balancing the role of that responsibility alongside the continuous pursuit of being an Author.

Formerly Katandra Shanel Jackson, Mrs. Nunnally resides in South East Georgia, where she shares a home with her children, two pups and her husband!

Carnal Sobriety is the Author's 6th published book to date.

Connect with 'Kat' at FreedomInk.
www.freedomink365.com/about_the_publisher

Enjoy this sneak peek excerpt from the upcoming book,
'Can't Raise No Man' by Katandra Jackson Nunnally.

First comes the baby in a baby carriage...

Oh to hell with love & marriage. I'm a married woman NOW sure enough. But my new status in life has not always been the case. I've had my unfair share of days of being husbandless. Left to rear children on my own, alone. No decent male role model around long enough to even be considered for the role of step-father. Application denied before one even bothered to fill one out. And they never did. Stick around long enough that is. Just a list of unimportant individuals whose names I've since forgotten. Boyfriend after boyfriend. All boys. All commitment-phobes! Each bearing his own fear. Fear of staying. Fear of being responsible. Fear of becoming a man. So I raised him on my own, alone!

Would you please quit sangin' that same old sad damn song...

"Oh you're just a woman. You can't raise no man. He need a daddy. Honey, where yo' husband at?" Every great aunt had that look in her eyes. Heaven thank you that the generations before me believed in getting married and staying married. Even if the wife was a miserable wreck and all the husband did was cause her grief with every child that was born outside of his marriage! Well now where is the 'Happily Ever After' in that? Okay so keep giving me them side eyes and on occasion ask the question, but would you please quit sangin' that same old sad damn song? I've heard it all before. "You can't raise no man!" The path I saw his father heading down was making a pretty bold statement of its own. 'Yes. You're going to have to raise this [man] child on your own!" Even before his lengthy departure, I was preparing to go it all alone.

Also Available at FreedomInk Publishing…

Darkness Before the Dawn by Dawn Miller

Jesus Paid It All: True Hero by Elder Steve Carter Jr.

Jareth, First Lord by Mellie Miller

The Lady, Niobe by Kenny L. Mitchell

Woman on Fire by Trinette Collier

Anybody's Somebody by Phoenix

Life & Love Through My Eyes by Ramona Jones

MOJO For Sale by Katandra Jackson Nunnally

The list goes on and on! Check out these amazing books and so many more.

WWW.FREEDOMINK365.COM

www.ingramcontent.com/pod-product-compliance
Lightning Source LLC
Chambersburg PA
CBHW020951030426
42339CB00004B/44